# TIME FOR A CHECKUP!

*by Sammy Horner*

CHRISTIAN FOCUS PUBLICATIONS

## WHAT'S INSIDE...

Published by Christian Focus Publications Ltd
Geanies House, Tain, Ross-shire, IV20 1TW
©1997 Sammy Horner

Illustrations by Tim Charnick, Profile Design

ISBN 1-85792-256-5

Our bodies are amazing!
Have you ever wondered how they work?
What keeps us alive, makes us think, or laugh?
Why do our bodies get sick or stop working?

Did you know there is one specialist Doctor
who is very interested in you? He wants to
make sure you're healthy and in good shape.

Read on and find out if you're as fit
as you thought...

# 1 'DOCTOR, DOCTOR, I FEEL LIKE A PAIR OF CURTAINS'

How many corny 'Doctor doctor' jokes have you heard? You know the kind...

'Doctor, doctor, I feel like a snooker ball'...
*'Well, get to the end of the queue!'*
or
'Doctor, doctor, people keep ignoring me'...
*'Next!'*

Oh dear...bad jokes about doctors seem to be endless, but how would you feel if your doctor really said those things? The fact is that doctors are there to help us get better when we are sick. They are able to deal with all kinds of situations. Doctors do their very best to help us.

Can you imagine what it would be like if doctors just told you to go home and pull yourself together? Things go wrong with people all the time, and it's then that we are glad to have doctors.

# - YOU CAN'T PULL YOURSELF TOGETHER

In a book called the Bible, we are told that something has gone wrong with every single person in the whole world. It's not really a disease, but it's very serious and it works in people's minds and bodies, just like an illness.

You won't find this 'illness' described in any medical book, in fact you won't even find the word, but you just need to look at the world around us to see that this problem is everywhere. The Bible calls it, 'sin', a teeny little word that has a big meaning for all of us.

In the same way as an illness shows itself in what doctors call symptoms, (like when your face gets spotty if you catch Chicken Pox!) so the Bible tells us about the symptoms of this worldwide epidemic! You can't always see sin in the same way as you might see the result of a broken arm or a swollen ankle...it affects us in a very different way.

Sin touches every part of us, our body, our mind and our feelings. It affects how we behave, our attitude to other people and even our attitude to God himself. Sin is such a nasty thing that it is the only thing about us that God hates.

The good news is that God loves people, but he sees how sin affects you and is willing to do whatever is necessary to get rid of it! He is like a great doctor who is willing to work with people who need cured...he hates the problem, but he loves the person.

**SYMPTOMS OF SIN**
greed
lies
stealing
violence
treating others badly...
selfishness
not caring for
people....
being ungrateful...
hatred
gossiping...

The symptoms can be seen in every single person. It seems to be more serious in some people, but every one has got them, and everyone is in need of help. Here are some of the symptoms of sin that the Bible mentions... do you have any?

There are even more, but you can see that all of us do some of these things from time to time. The fact is that we can't just pull ourselves together, we need help!

**HELP!**

**SYMPTOMS OF SIN**
greed
lies
stealing
violence
treating others badly...
selfishness
not caring for people...
being ungrateful
hatred
gossiping...

The Bible tells us that God knew all about this problem and decided to do something about it. His plan was incredible, and involved God coming into this world as a man - he was called Jesus. He wants to help and he can help, no matter how badly sin has damaged you.

You can read how God became a man in the Bible in the part called 'Matthew', chapter 1 verses 18 - 25.

In the book of Matthew you can also find Jesus compared to a doctor.

Look in chapter 9 and verse 12...if you can't find it ask someone to help you look it up.

# HELP FROM A REAL SPECIALIST!

Just about everything that needs fixed has a specialist 'fixer'. We have already said that doctors help fix our bodies, so how come as soon as we find out that there is a problem with every single person in the world we don't go to the best doctor of all? No one else in history has been able to sort out this problem of sin...no one, except Jesus that is!

The thing about doctors is that they understand how people's bodies work and what needs to be done to sort the problem... they know what all the bits do. They understand what makes it tick! The Bible tells us that God made human beings. He knows how our bodies work and he knows what is best for us.

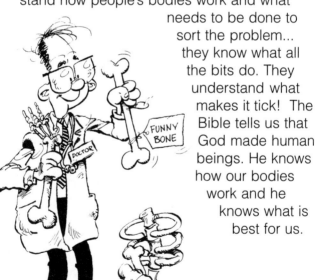

When God became a man, he also understood the kinds of problems that we have as human beings, because he went through them as well. Did you know that Jesus knew what it was like to:

## FEEL HUNGRY AND THIRSTY

## HAVE FRIENDS DISAPPOINT HIM

## FEEL LONELY

## FEEL SLEEPY

## GET HURT

## BE ACCUSED OF THINGS HE DIDN'T DO

## AND LOADS OF OTHER THINGS...

He knew what it was like to feel under pressure. Jesus not only knows what we need, but he understands what it's like to live in this world. The really amazing thing about Jesus is that even though he had real pressure put on him to give into sin...he never did.

Jesus is the only person in all history to live without any sin in his life. In the same way that doctors are qualified to treat our illnesses, Jesus is qualified to deal with our problem of sin because of who he is and what he has done.

# SICK TO THE BACK TEETH!

So how serious is this problem? How does it affect you? Can you recognise the symptoms in your own life?

The Bible tells us that every single person has certain things about them that reminds us that God made human beings. We feel a certain way if we see other people suffering. Feelings of sympathy, care and being fair all come from God 'cause that's what he is like. Jesus was the most caring, loving, fair minded person who ever lived, and that is how we are meant to be.

Let's take a look at what the Bible says about the parts of us that sin has affected:

our imagination

our mind

our relationship with others

our motives

our actions and deeds

our relationship with Jesus

You see **why** we do things is just as important as doing those good things. Sin causes us trouble in many ways!

Now because you are a sinner doesn't mean that you are completely horrible and slobber n' scream n' rant n' rave!

It does mean however, that you are not everything that God wanted you to be. It means that your relationship with God is damaged and that sin can get a stronger hold on you. It touches everything that people are involved in. The question is...what are we going to do about it?

# 4 THE HEALING PROCESS

Just as the Bible tells us about the symptoms of sin, it also clearly shows us the *only* cure.

Jesus was so concerned about our sins that he showed us how we should live - he also did something incredible!

He knew that our sin stopped us from being friends with God. Jesus was accused of all kinds of terrible things that he wasn't guilty of.

> **He was called:**
> *a liar, a greedy man,*
> *a drunk, a terrorist,*
> *a fraud, a devil*
> *a man who made friends*
> *with dangerous,*
> *dirty, cheating*
> *and violent people.*

Although none of this was true, Jesus was accused and killed on a cross.

This seems like bad news, and in a way it is certainly sad news, but it's also good news. God let his Son Jesus die on the cross. Why?

Jesus was completely innocent and yet he took the punishment for all the bad stuff we have mentioned...and even more! When we become aware of how much God loves us, and all that he has done for us, we start to understand how bad sin is. We begin to see that our sins have been hurting others and offending God.

It's like all the bad stuff anyone has ever done was dealt with by Jesus. So now when a person believes in Jesus, God doesn't accuse or blame them for being greedy or lying, because his own innocent Son died for everyone who has done those things.

**JESUS DIED FOR**

My Sin

It's a bit like someone else paying a bill for you...you don't have to pay for what you've done wrong in God's sight ( although doing wrong things sometimes has consequences for the future). All you have to do is accept what Jesus did for you!

# WE'LL START WITH THE HEART!

Gary wasn't a bad lad...just a bit of a joker. He always made fun of everything. When the circus had a parade through town Gary made jokes about everything. Three camels went by in procession, Gary shouted, 'Hi there Humphry...geddit? Hump three!' All the lads laughed.

The clowns came by next. When they were giving out noses, those guys thought that they said 'roses' and asked for really big red ones! Do ya get it?...Roses and noses... The guys giggled!

Later in the supermarket he asked the man behind the counter for a box of Ten o'clock mints.

'Don't you mean *After Eights?*' asked the man.

'Same thing' said Gary, 'ten o'clock is after eight isn't it? Do ya get it? Ten...after eight?' His chums chuckled!

The only time that Gary couldn't make a joke was when *she* was around. She was the cutest girl in the whole solar system. She had short dark hair, always dressed really cool, had a smile that would melt the North Pole...her name was Hazel and so were her eyes! Every time she appeared Gary went all dopey. He got all his words back to front and upside down. 'Happy to see you' became 'Hippy to sneeze you'. 'You're looking rather nice today!' ended up sounding like, 'You're cooking father's rice today!'

'Oh no,' thought Gary as he saw Hazel walking towards him, 'I always sound like such a twit when I try to talk to her... and to make things worse my mates are here!'

Wee Tommy and Colin braced themselves for the biggest laugh of the day...they knew how Gary spoke whenever he saw Hazel.

'C'mon now,' Gary thought to himself. 'How hard can it be to say, 'Hi Hazel...where are you off to?' The words were right in his mind. He rehearsed them over and over as Hazel drew closer and closer, then, just as he was about to speak she

went and did it...she smiled at him!

'Hiz Hizil...pears are soft too! Doooh!' Colin creased in two while Tommy laughed so hard that a big bubble appeared out of his nose. Gary went really red! Hazel ignored the two boys, smiled at Gary and said one word.

'Youth Club.'

15

'Youth Club!' said all three lads together. 'Boring!' they yapped. 'It's in the old church hall!'

Gary was just about to tell his daft church joke, 'Why do churches have steeples? So that everyone can see the point!' when he remembered that he'd probably get it wrong while still in the vicinity of the Hazel Zone!

'You can come if you want to,' said Hazel.

Gary wasn't interested in church much...but he was interested in Hazel!

Tommy and Colin laughed and giggled while Gary desperately tried to think of a way to suggest that they follow Hazel to church...and still look cool!

'Let's go for a laugh!' suggested Gary. 'We can make fun of everything at church!'

Tommy and Colin agreed.

It wasn't what they expected, lots of people their age, loud music, videos and flashing lights.

Between the music and videos, some guy spoke about stuff like faith and Jesus but he didn't speak for very long, so the boys listened. Gary didn't want to look too interested, and so he waited for the best moment to make a wise crack. Hazel was far enough away to stop his words getting twisted, so Gary waited and waited and waited.

'It's important that we allow Jesus to have our heart,' said the between videos guy.

'No thanks !' yelled Gary, 'I don't fancy the operation much!'

Colin nearly choked on his cherry coke, while Tommy's face screwed up so much with laughter that Gary thought that he looked as if he had a fold away head!

16

Only the three boys laughed, the rest of the room was so quiet that you could have heard a spider burp!

A video burst into life and the programme continued without any more dumb comments.

On the way out, the guy was saying good-bye to everyone at the door. Gary got closer and nervous all at the same time. Just as he reached the door and expected a good telling off, the guy said, 'So you don't fancy the operation then? You think that giving your heart to someone involves surgery, do you?'

'What else could it mean?' asked Gary. 'Everyone knows that your heart is just a pump that squirts blood around your body. It's just a bloodpump!'

Tommy and Colin never made a sound, but their shoulders went up and down .

'And fathermear,' continued Gary, 'hi don't stink bat chew half the write doo smell us fat to chew...errr...to do!' It was happening again...Hazel had to be close. Sure enough, there she was only three feet away.

'Oh no, I'm done for,' thought Gary.

The guy saw Gary's reaction to Hazel and began

to speak again.

'Just imagine for a moment that you really liked a girl. Imagine that you and she went for a long romantic walk through a beautiful field of wheat, and then down beside the river!'

Gary got even redder than before. First his neck, then his ears, then his whole head. From a distance, with his white Tee-shirt and big red head, he looked a bit like a match stick! The guy went on.

'As you get down to the river you take a little diamond ring from your pocket, look deep into the girl's big brown eyes...'

Gary glanced at Hazel...he could feel a big drip of sweat dangling from his nose...at least he hoped it was sweat!

'... and just as you are about to put it on her finger she pulls her hand away and says, "Haven't you got anything to say first?"

'With all your might, you think through your most romantic proposal and with all the passion you can muster you say... 'Darling... I really love you with all my bloodpump!'

Everyone laughed, even Gary thought that the guy was pretty funny.

The guy went on, 'You see, to give your heart to

someone is a great act of faith. You are saying that you trust that person completely. That you know that they will not hurt you or misuse you.

'Everybody needs their bloodpump heart to live, but to say that we trust someone with our heart, or that we love someone with our heart, or even that we will give our heart to someone really means that we are ready to dedicate ourselves to that person for ever...it means that you are going to give your all to that person...that is how we need to give ourselves to Jesus!'

'I geddit,' said Gary, 'I Geddit!'

Sometimes you may hear other people who believe in Jesus using all kinds of words and expressions that you don't understand. It's OK to ask what they are talking about.

Remember that the story of Jesus is a Love story. It's all about the fact that God loved us *so much* that he was willing to let Jesus give his life to help us understand his love for us. When you see it like that, it's not surprising that we often use words like, 'Giving our heart to God.' We just mean that we are now devoted to the God who really loves us.

# 6 CHECKUP FROM THE NECK UP!

We've already talked about 'the heart', but what about the mind? The things that we think about are really important.

Jesus said that if we...

**Nº1 LOVE GOD**

**Nº2 LOVE OTHER PEOPLE**

Then we are keeping the two most important commands in the world!

He said that loving God means using our mind, as well as our emotions, feelings and bodies. It is very important that we use our brain when we decide to do what God says! We use our mind to help us make decisions.

God's ideas on how people should think and behave are often very different to our own ideas. Imagine what the world would be like if people thought the same way as God! Imagine a world in which people loved their enemies.

God wants to help you see people and life in a new way. This new way of thinking may seem strange to other people. It's like a complete turn around from the normal way of life, but God tells us in the Bible that his way is always the best way! To be fair, sympathetic, caring, brave, helpful, loving and kind is more like how God intended people to be.

An ordinary doctor checks us out to make sure everything is working OK.

We need to allow God to check out what we are watching, listening to, getting involved in and what we are putting into our minds.

God wants to be involved in **all** of our life. He may want to change some of it, ask us to do new things that we have never thought about or to be careful about what we say and do.

In the same way as we trust our doctor to get us back in shape, we need to trust God to remove anything that may cause damage or harm.

# BREATHE DEEPLY!

Every animal in the world breathes...they have to otherwise they wouldn't be alive! People need to breathe as well, but did you know that human beings are not just another animal!

At the very beginning of the Bible in a book called Genesis, we find the story of God's amazing creation. We are told that God gave everything life, but when he made human beings, he did something different. He said that men and women would be made in his image. I don't think that means that God looks like us physically, but rather that he gave us certain things that make us something like him.

Do you ever wonder why we feel sad when we watch news reports on TV? Why we cry at pictures of hungry people? Why we want to see people treated fairly and get annoyed when they are not? Well that's how God made us.

The Bible says that God took great care over his creation, but that he took a special interest in human beings...in fact one part of the story says that God 'breathed life into the man'.

If we want to follow God, we still struggle with sin and do wrong things, but God has promised to help us. When we become a Christian we are filled with God's Holy Spirit. He is there to comfort, guide and teach us throughout our whole life. Having God's Spirit is as important for living as having breath in our lungs.

Although we cannot see the Spirit of God, the Bible promises us that he is with Christians all the time. He helps us to decide what is good or bad. He helps us see life in a new way.

It's like God himself has come to live with us, and he wants to be involved in everything that we do. He has promised to help us make sense of the Bible, to point out the kind of things that could harm us, and to be a wise friend who never leaves us.

# STARTING A FULL RECOVERY!

Finding out how much God has done for us can make us feel really great grateful, but it can also make us feel sad that Jesus was treated so badly because of our wrong doing. Understanding these two things is the start of a full recovery.

Being grateful to God and understanding how much he loves you makes him very happy. To hear you say that you are sorry for all the rotten things that you have done is the best and most exciting thing that God ever hears from a person.

Talking to God is called prayer. It's best if you talk to God in your own words and tell him

how you feel...that way you know what you mean...and so does God!

Admitting to God that you are sorry for your sins and want to live his way, means you are asking God to help you start a whole new way of life, as a follower of Jesus.

When we start listening to God, with the help of his Spirit, we try to stop doing, thinking and feeling wrong things, and begin to start thinking, feeling and doing what is right.

Now remember that it is a lifetime process and nobody is perfect. We may be tempted to go back to our old way of thinking, feeling and doing. Ask God to help you! Don't worry, God still loves you, forgives you and is still your friend.

To find out more about God and the life he wants for you, get a Bible. There are lots of different versions...
even some for kids with nice easy words. There are also lots of videos of Bible stories, *books, magazines, CD's, tapes, activity packs and even some computer games that can help you understand more about living the way that God wants you to.

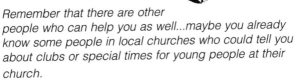

*Remember that there are other people who can help you as well...maybe you already know some people in local churches who could tell you about clubs or special times for young people at their church.*

*\* Look out for the second book in this series, **Grow Up!***

# STRONG MEDICINE

Every bit of your body has its own special part to play in keeping you in good condition. If one part doesn't work, well then the whole body suffers.

A man in the Bible called Paul once described all the people who love God as a body...he asks us to think about some funny ideas he had.

He said, 'Imagine your whole body was made up of only one enormous eyeball! How could you smell things if this was the case?'

Paul was telling us that all the people who believe in Jesus need to act as if they are all a part of one body... everyone is important and has a special job to do to make sure that the whole body stays in shape!

This is good news for us, 'cause it means that we are all very special and have an important role to play.

**You might be:**
*a good speaker,*
*a good listener,*
*musical or artistic,*
*very clever,*
*or wonderfully simple,*
*good at making things*
*with your hands,*
*or solving problems*
*with your mind...*

Whatever you can do, it's needed by someone else and God can use your particular function to help others!

People who are a part of this body are called the 'church' and the church is full of lots of different kinds of people.

When we start with the heart, and dedicate ourselves to Jesus, we find that the next thing that he wants us to do is to become dedicated to other people.

If our body is made up of all kinds of different people with different skills and talents then we should be able to help just about every kind of person in the world!

God really thinks about the best ways to help people! What are you good at? Are you working as well as you can or should be? If a body is to be strong and healthy then all its members and organs need to be working together properly.

Every part of this body is important to God, and important for other people...
**You** are a very important part of the church.

## 10 BODY BUILDING

We have discovered that we needed God's help to cure our sin. Now it's time to realise that we must have regular checkups to make sure that we remain healthy.

In the same way that someone recovering from an illness must be taken care of, so we need to look after our new life. The Bible tells us that there are some things that we need to do to stay in shape.

*Reading the Bible* is important because we find instructions on the best way to live, the kind of things to avoid and what we should be involved in. The Bible also gives us good examples of people who lived for God, and the kind of problems they overcame.

*Praying* is also important. It lets us speak to God about anything at all, we can thank him, say we are sorry, ask him to help us or others. Just as you talk freely with a friend, God wants you to speak openly to him.

Another important exercise is to **meet together with others who love Jesus**.

*This means that we can:*
thank God together,
make friends,
talk about things that
we don't understand,
and help each other through
difficult times.

When people meet together, we usually call this 'church'. By reading, praying, listening, talking, thinking and living like Jesus did, we can become more and more like him.

Finally, the Bible tells us that it is important to *let others know about Jesus* in the things that we say and the things that we do.

You have some very good news for other people who don't know about sin and all that it can do. Don't be frightened to tell them and show them what Jesus has done for you, and what he can

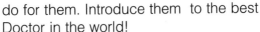

do for them. Introduce them to the best Doctor in the world!

For God loved the world so much that he gave his only Son, so that every-one who believes in him may not die but have eternal life.
*John 3:16*

Jesus makes a special promise to all those that love him. Even though our human body eventually gets worn out, everyone who has faith in Jesus will be with him in heaven. What other doctor can say that?